my itty-bitty bio

Anne Frank

Cherry Lake Press

Published in the United States of America by Cherry Lake Publishing
Ann Arbor, Michigan
www.cherrylakepublishing.com

Reading Adviser: Beth Walker Gambro, MS, Ed., Reading Consultant, Yorkville, IL
Illustrator: Leo Trinidad

Photo Credits: Photo Collection Anne Frank Stichting, 5, 13, 15; Library of Congress, 7; Courtesy of the United States Holocaust Memorial Museum, 9; © IanDagnall Computing / Alamy Stock Photo, 11, 22; © Sergi Reboredo / VWPics via AP Images, 17; Nationaal Archief Author Jack de Nijs for Anefo, 19; © Pictorial Press Ltd / Alamy Stock Photo, 21, 23

Cherry Lake Press is an imprint of Cherry Lake Publishing Group

Library of Congress Cataloging-in-Publication Data has been filed and is available at catalog.loc.gov.

Printed in the United States of America

table of contents

About the author: Meeg Pincus is the award-winning author of 30 nonfiction picture books. She has worked for newspapers, book publishers, universities—and, years ago, at Disneyland. Meeg lives with her family in California, where she loves to write, read, make art, and sing.

About the illustrator: Leo Trinidad is a NY Times bestselling comic book artist, illustrator, and animator from Costa Rica. For more than 12 years he's been creating content for children's books and TV shows. Leo created the first animated series ever produced in Central America, and founded Rocket Cartoons, one of the most successful animation studios in Latin America. He is also the 2018 winner of the Central American Graphic Novel contest.

my story

I was born in Germany in 1929. My family was **Jewish**.

We had a nice home, food, books, and toys.

When I was 4, my family left Germany.

The country's cruel **leader** did not like Jewish people.

In my new home, I loved school and parties. The cruel leader started a **war**.

But I still had a fun, happy life.

I got a **diary** for my birthday. I wrote about my dreams of peace and joy.

I hoped someday my words could become a book!

What do you hope for?

Then the war came to our country. Soldiers sent Jewish people away to **prison camps**.

My family had to hide.

We hid in secret rooms for many months. We stayed quiet.

We had little food or fresh air.

How would you feel hiding like that?

One morning, we were found.
Soldiers took us away.

A kind helper saved my diary.

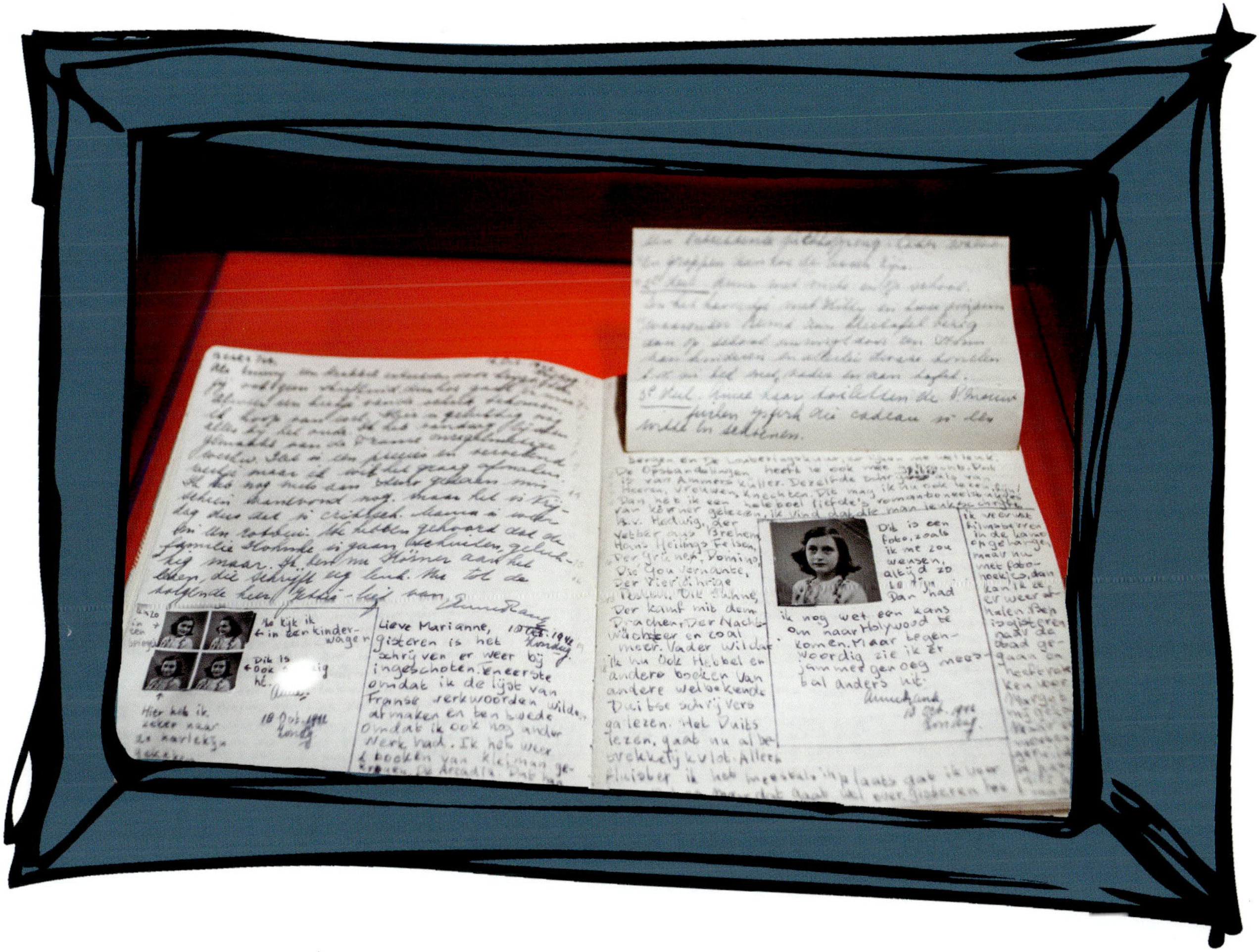
Lieve Marianne,
Dit is een foto, zoals ik me zou wensen, altijd zo te zijn. Dan had ik nog wel een kans om naar Holywood te komen. Maar tegenwoordig zie ik er jammer genoeg meestal anders uit.

In a prison camp, I got sick and died. So did my mother and sister.

After the war, the kind helper gave my father my diary.

My diary became a **famous** book.

Today, people around the world still read my words of hope and peace.

What would you like to ask me?

timeline

1942

1860

1947

1960

Born
1929

Died
1945

glossary & index

glossary

diary (DIE-uh-ree) a written record of personal thoughts and feelings

famous (FAY-muhs) known by many people

Jewish (JOO-ish) relating to the religion of Judaism or its followers

leader (LEE-duhr) a person who guides others

prison camps (PRIH-zuhn KAMPS) a place where a government holds people it dislikes

war (WOR) a fight between nations or other opposing forces

index